Contents

Lemon Honey Chicken and Stuffing

MAKES: 6 servings   **PREP:** 15 minutes   **BAKE:** 1 hour

1¾ cups SWANSON® Chicken Stock

  2 medium carrots, shredded (about 1 cup)

  4 cups PEPPERIDGE FARM® Herb Seasoned Stuffing

  6 bone-in chicken breast halves, skin removed

  2 tablespoons honey

  2 tablespoons lemon juice

  1 tablespoon chopped fresh parsley *or* 1 teaspoon dried parsley flakes

  3 lemon slices, cut in half

1. Heat the stock and carrots in a 3-quart saucepan over medium heat to a boil. Remove the saucepan from the heat. Add the stuffing and mix lightly.

2. Spoon the stuffing mixture into a greased 3-quart shallow baking dish. Top with the chicken.

3. Bake at 375°F. for 50 minutes.

4. Stir the honey, lemon juice and parsley in a small bowl. Brush the chicken with the honey mixture. Place the lemon slices onto the chicken. Bake for 10 minutes or until the chicken is cooked through.

Chicken, Broccoli, Mushroom & Brown Rice Bake

MAKES: 4 servings   **PREP:** 10 minutes   **BAKE:** 45 minutes

- 1   carton (18.3 ounces) CAMPBELL'S® V8® Garden Broccoli Soup
- ¼   cup water
- ¾   cup *uncooked* instant brown rice
- 4   ounces mushrooms, sliced (about 1½ cups)
- 1   large onion, chopped (about 1 cup)
- 4   skinless, boneless chicken breast halves (about 1 pound)
      Paprika
      Ground black pepper

1. Heat the oven to 375°F.

2. Stir the soup, water, rice, mushrooms and onion in a 2-quart shallow baking dish. Top with the chicken. Sprinkle the chicken with the paprika and black pepper. Cover the baking dish.

3. Bake for 45 minutes or until the chicken is cooked through and the rice is tender.

Chicken & Stuffing with Vegetables

MAKES: 6 servings　　**PREP:** 15 minutes　　**BAKE:** 30 minutes

- **1 can (10¾ ounces) CAMPBELL'S® Condensed Cream of Mushroom Soup (Regular or 98% Fat Free)**
- **1 cup milk or water**
- **2 cups frozen vegetable combination (broccoli, cauliflower, carrots)**
- **2 cups cubed cooked chicken or turkey**
- **4 cups PEPPERIDGE FARM® Herb Seasoned Stuffing**
- **1 cup shredded Swiss cheese or Cheddar cheese**

1. In large saucepan mix soup, milk and vegetables. Over medium-high heat, heat to a boil. Remove from heat. Add chicken and stuffing. Mix lightly. Spoon into 2-quart shallow baking dish.

2. Bake at 350°F. for 25 minutes or until hot.

3. Sprinkle cheese over chicken mixture. Bake 5 minutes more or until cheese is melted.

tip

*For **2 cups** cubed cooked chicken: In medium saucepan over medium heat, in **4 cups** boiling water, cook **1 pound** skinless, boneless chicken breasts **or** thighs, cubed, 5 minutes or until chicken is cooked through.*

Baked Italian Chicken & Pasta

MAKES: 4 servings   **PREP:** 5 minutes   **BAKE:** 45 minutes

  1   can (10¾ ounces) CAMPBELL'S® Condensed Tomato Soup
1⅓ cups water
  1   teaspoon dried basil leaves, crushed
  2   cups *uncooked* corkscrew-shaped pasta (rotini)
  4   skinless, boneless chicken breast halves (about 1 pound)
  ½   cup shredded mozzarella cheese

1. Stir the soup, water, basil and pasta in a 2-quart shallow baking dish. Top with the chicken. Sprinkle with the cheese and additional basil, if desired. Cover the baking dish.

2. Bake at 350°F. for 45 minutes or until the chicken is cooked through and the pasta is tender.

Super Chicken Casserole

MAKES: 8 servings	PREP: 15 minutes	BAKE: 25 minutes

- ½ cup PEPPERIDGE FARM® Herb Seasoned Stuffing, crushed
- 2 tablespoons grated Parmesan cheese
- 2 tablespoons butter, melted
- 1 can (10¾ ounces) CAMPBELL'S® Condensed Cream of Broccoli Soup (Regular *or* 98% Fat Free)
- 1 cup milk
- ½ cup shredded mozzarella cheese
- ¼ teaspoon garlic powder
- ⅛ teaspoon ground black pepper
- 1 cup elbow macaroni, cooked and drained
- 2 cups cubed cooked chicken *or* turkey
- 1 package (10 ounces) frozen peas and carrots, cooked and drained

1. Heat the oven to 400°F. Stir the stuffing, Parmesan cheese and butter in a medium bowl.

2. Stir the soup, milk, mozzarella cheese, garlic powder and black pepper in a 2-quart baking dish. Stir in the macaroni, chicken and peas and carrots.

3. Bake for 20 minutes or until the chicken mixture is hot and bubbling. Stir the chicken mixture. Sprinkle with the stuffing mixture.

4. Bake for 5 minutes or until the stuffing mixture is golden brown.

Sweet Zesty Chicken

MAKES: 6 servings   **PREP:** 10 minutes   **BAKE:** 1 hour

- 6 **bone-in chicken breast halves (about 3 pounds)**
- ½ **teaspoon garlic powder**
- 2 **cups PREGO® Traditional Italian Sauce *or* Marinara Italian Sauce**
- ¼ **cup soy sauce**
- 3 **tablespoons Worcestershire sauce**
- ½ **cup honey**
- 1 **large onion, chopped (about 1 cup)**
- 6 **cups hot cooked rice**

1. Place the chicken in a 3-quart shallow baking dish. Sprinkle the chicken with the garlic powder. Bake at 375°F. for 30 minutes. Pour off any fat.

2. Stir the Italian sauce, soy sauce, Worcestershire sauce, honey and onion in a medium bowl. Pour over the chicken and bake for 30 minutes or until chicken is cooked through. Remove the chicken from the dish. Stir the sauce. Serve with the rice.

Broccoli Fish Bake

MAKES: 4 servings   **PREP:** 15 minutes   **BAKE:** 20 minutes

1 **package (about 10 ounces) frozen broccoli spears, cooked and drained**

4 **fresh *or* thawed frozen firm white fish fillets (cod, haddock *or* halibut) (about 1 pound)**

1 **can (10¾ ounces) CAMPBELL'S® Condensed Cream of Broccoli Soup**

⅓ **cup milk**

¼ **cup shredded Cheddar cheese**

2 **tablespoons dry bread crumbs**

1 **teaspoon butter, melted**

⅛ **teaspoon paprika**

1. Place the broccoli into a 2-quart shallow baking dish. Top with the fish. Stir the soup and milk in a small bowl. Pour the soup mixture over the fish. Sprinkle with the cheese.

2. Stir the bread crumbs, butter and paprika in a small bowl. Sprinkle the crumb mixture over all.

3. Bake at 450°F. for 20 minutes or until the fish flakes easily when tested with a fork.

tip

*You can substitute **1 pound** fresh broccoli spears, cooked and drained, for the frozen.*

Pasta, Cheese & Vegetable Casserole

MAKES: 5 servings   **PREP:** 20 minutes   **BAKE:** 50 minutes

- 1 can (10¾ ounces) CAMPBELL'S® Condensed Cream of Chicken Soup (Regular *or* 98% Fat Free) *or* Condensed Cream of Celery Soup
- 1½ cups milk
- ½ teaspoon ground black pepper
- 1½ cups shredded reduced-fat Cheddar cheese (about 6 ounces)
- 1½ cups frozen mixed vegetables
- 4 cups corkscrew-shaped pasta (rotini), cooked and drained
- ⅓ cup crushed corn flakes

1. Stir the soup, milk, black pepper, cheese, vegetables and pasta in a 2½-quart casserole.

2. Bake at 400°F. for 30 minutes or until the pasta mixture is hot and bubbling. Stir the pasta mixture. Sprinkle with the corn flakes.

3. Bake for 20 minutes or until the cornflakes are golden brown.

Baked Ziti

MAKES: 4 servings   **PREP:** 25 minutes   **BAKE:** 30 minutes

  1   jar (24 ounces) PREGO® Traditional Italian Sauce *or* Roasted Garlic & Herb Italian Sauce
1½ cups shredded mozzarella cheese
  5   cups tube-shaped pasta (ziti), cooked and drained
  ¼   cup grated Parmesan cheese

1. Stir the Italian sauce, **1 cup** mozzarella cheese and ziti in a large bowl. Spoon the mixture into a 2-quart shallow baking dish. Sprinkle with the remaining mozzarella cheese and Parmesan cheese.

2. Bake at 350°F. for 30 minutes or until the mixture is hot and bubbling.

tips

To freeze, prepare the ziti but do not bake. Cover it tightly with foil and freeze. Bake frozen ziti, uncovered, at 350°F. for 1 hour or until hot and bubbling. Or, refrigerate frozen ziti for 24 hours to thaw. Bake thawed ziti, uncovered, at 350°F. for 45 minutes or until hot and bubbling.

For 8 servings, double the recipe. Spoon into a 3-quart shallow baking dish and bake for 45 minutes or until hot and bubbling.

Neapolitan Pasta Shells

MAKES: 4 servings   **PREP:** 20 minutes   **BAKE:** 30 minutes

- 2 **tablespoons vegetable oil**
- 2 **medium zucchini, sliced (about 3 cups)**
- 2 **cups sliced mushrooms**
- 1 **medium onion, chopped (about ½ cup)**
- ¼ **teaspoon ground black pepper**
- 2 **cups PREGO® Three Cheese Italian Sauce**
- ½ **of a 16-ounce package medium shell-shaped pasta, cooked and drained (4 cups)**
- 1 **cup shredded mozzarella cheese**

1. Heat the oil in a 3-quart saucepan over medium heat. Add the zucchini, mushrooms, onion and pepper and cook until the vegetables are tender-crisp.

2. Stir the Italian sauce and pasta in the saucepan. Spoon into a 2-quart baking dish. Sprinkle with the cheese.

3. Bake at 350°F. for 30 minutes or until hot and bubbling.

Extra-Easy Spinach Lasagna

MAKES: 8 servings   **PREP:** 20 minutes   **BAKE:** 50 minutes   **STAND:** 10 minutes

1 container (15 ounces) ricotta cheese
1 package (10 ounces) frozen chopped spinach, thawed and well drained
8 ounces shredded mozzarella cheese (about 2 cups)
1 jar (24 ounces) PREGO® Fresh Mushroom Italian Sauce
6 *uncooked* lasagna noodles
¼ cup water

1. Stir the ricotta cheese, spinach and **1 cup** mozzarella cheese in a medium bowl.

2. Spread **1 cup** Italian sauce in a 2-quart shallow baking dish. Top with **3** lasagna noodles and **half** the spinach mixture. Repeat the layers. Top with the remaining sauce. Slowly pour water around the inside edges of the baking dish. **Cover.**

3. Bake at 400°F. for 40 minutes. Uncover the dish. Sprinkle with the remaining mozzarella cheese. Bake for 10 minutes or until it's hot and bubbling. Let stand for 10 minutes.

tip ||||||||||||||||||||||||||||||||||

To thaw the spinach, microwave on HIGH for 3 minutes, breaking apart with a fork halfway through heating.

Mac & Cheese Veggie Bake

MAKES: 6 servings   **PREP:** 20 minutes   **BAKE:** 30 minutes

- 2 cans (10¾ ounces *each*) CAMPBELL'S® Condensed Cheddar Cheese Soup
- 1½ cups milk
- 2 tablespoons Dijon-style mustard
- 1½ cups frozen sugar snap peas
- 1 medium green *or* red pepper, diced (about 1 cup)
- 3 cups elbow macaroni, cooked and drained
- ¼ cup water
- 2 tablespoons butter, melted
- 4 cups PEPPERIDGE FARM® Corn Bread Stuffing

1. Stir the soup, milk, mustard, snap peas, pepper and macaroni in a 3-quart shallow baking dish.

2. Stir the water and butter in a large bowl. Add the stuffing and mix lightly to coat. Sprinkle the stuffing over the macaroni mixture.

3. Bake at 400°F. for 30 minutes or until it's hot and bubbling.

Mexi-Corn Lasagna

MAKES: 8 servings   **PREP:** 20 minutes   **BAKE:** 30 minutes   **STAND:** 10 minutes

- 1 **container (16 ounces) cottage cheese**
- 2 **eggs, beaten**
- ¼ **cup grated Parmesan cheese**
- 1 **teaspoon dried oregano leaves, crushed**
- 1 **pound ground beef**
- 1 **can (15 ounces) tomato sauce**
- 1 **cup PACE® Picante Sauce**
- 1 **tablespoon chili powder**
- 1 **cup frozen whole kernel corn**
- 12 **corn tortillas (6-inch)**
- 4 **ounces shredded Cheddar cheese (about 1 cup)**

1. Stir the cottage cheese, eggs, Parmesan cheese and oregano in a medium bowl.

2. Cook the beef in a 10-inch skillet over medium-high heat until it's well browned, stirring often to separate the meat. Pour off any fat. Stir the tomato sauce, picante sauce, chili powder and corn in the skillet. Heat through.

3. Arrange **6** tortillas in the bottom and up the sides of a 3-quart shallow baking dish. Top with **half** of the beef mixture. Spoon the cottage cheese mixture over all. Top with the remaining tortillas and beef mixture.

4. Bake at 400°F. for 30 minutes or until it's hot and bubbling. Sprinkle with the Cheddar cheese. Let stand for 10 minutes. Serve with additional picante sauce.

Monterey Chicken Tortilla Casserole

MAKES: 4 servings   **PREP:** 15 minutes   **BAKE:** 40 minutes

- 1 cup coarsely crumbled tortilla chips
- 2 cups cubed cooked chicken *or* turkey
- 1 can (about 15 ounces) cream-style corn
- ¾ cup PACE® Picante Sauce
- ½ cup sliced pitted ripe olives
- 2 ounces shredded Cheddar cheese (about ½ cup)
  Chopped green *or* red pepper
  Tortilla chips

1. Layer the crumbled chips, chicken, corn and picante sauce in a 1-quart casserole. Top with the olives and cheese.

2. Bake at 350°F. for 40 minutes or until the mixture is hot and bubbling. Top with the pepper. Serve with the chips.

Mediterranean Chicken Casserole

MAKES: 4 servings	**PREP:** 20 minutes	**BAKE:** 30 minutes

- 1 can (10¾ ounces) CAMPBELL'S® Condensed Cream of Celery Soup (Regular *or* 98% Fat Free)
- ½ cup water
- ½ teaspoon dried oregano leaves, crushed
- ¼ teaspoon ground black pepper
- 1 package (10 ounces) frozen chopped spinach, thawed and well-drained
- 2 cups cubed cooked chicken
- ⅔ cup orzo pasta, cooked and drained
- ½ cup shredded Italian cheese blend

1. Stir the soup, water, oregano, black pepper, spinach, chicken and pasta in a 2-quart shallow baking dish. Cover the baking dish.

2. Bake at 375°F. for 30 minutes or until the chicken mixture is hot and bubbling. Sprinkle with the cheese.

tip

You can substitute ***3 cans*** *(4.5 ounces* ***each****) SWANSON® Premium White Chunk Chicken Breast in Water, drained, for the cubed cooked chicken.*

Fiesta Chicken and Rice Bake

MAKES: 4 servings   **PREP:** 5 minutes   **BAKE:** 45 minutes

- 1   can (10¾ ounces) CAMPBELL'S® Condensed Tomato Soup
- ¾   cup water*
- ¾   cup **uncooked** regular long-grain white rice
- 1   teaspoon chili powder
- 4   skinless, boneless chicken breast halves (about 1 pound)
- ¼   cup shredded Cheddar cheese

For creamier rice, increase the water to 1⅓ cups.

1. Stir the soup, water, rice and chili powder in a 2-quart shallow baking dish. Place the chicken on the rice mixture. Sprinkle with additional chili powder, if desired. Cover the baking dish.

2. Bake at 375°F. for 45 minutes or until the chicken is cooked through and the rice is tender. Sprinkle with the cheese.

Meatloaf and Vegetables

MAKES: 6 servings   **PREP:** 25 minutes   **BAKE:** 1 hour

- 1½ **pounds ground beef**
- 2 **cans (10¾ ounces** *each***) CAMPBELL'S® Condensed Tomato Soup**
- ½ **cup dry bread crumbs**
- 1 **tablespoon Worcestershire sauce**
- ⅛ **teaspoon ground black pepper**
- 1 **egg, beaten**
- 1 **small onion, finely chopped**
- 6 **medium potatoes, cut into quarters**
- 6 **medium carrots, cut into 2-inch pieces**
- ¾ **cup water**

1. Thoroughly mix the beef, ½ **cup** soup, bread crumbs, Worcestershire, black pepper, egg and onion in a large bowl. Shape the beef mixture into an 8×4-inch loaf in a 13×9×2-inch baking pan. Arrange the potatoes and carrots around meatloaf in the baking pan.

2. Bake at 375°F. for 30 minutes. Spoon off any fat.

3. Stir the remaining soup and water in a small bowl. Spoon the soup mixture over the meatloaf and vegetables. Bake for 30 minutes or until the meatloaf is cooked through and the vegetables are fork-tender.

Baked Ziti Supreme

MAKES: 6 servings   **PREP:** 25 minutes   **BAKE:** 30 minutes

   1 **pound ground beef**
   1 **medium onion, chopped (about ½ cup)**
   1 **jar (24 ounces) PREGO® Fresh Mushroom Italian Sauce**
1½ **cups shredded mozzarella cheese (6 ounces)**
   5 **cups medium tube-shaped pasta (ziti), cooked and drained**
  ¼ **cup grated Parmesan cheese**

1. Cook the beef and onion in a 4-quart saucepan over medium-high heat until the beef is well browned, stirring often to separate the meat. Pour off any fat.

2. Stir the Italian sauce, **1 cup** mozzarella cheese and pasta in the saucepan. Spoon the mixture into a 3-quart shallow baking dish. Sprinkle with the remaining mozzarella cheese and Parmesan cheese. Bake at 350°F. for 30 minutes or until hot and bubbling.

Beef and Cornbread Bake

MAKES: 6 servings   **PREP:** 15 minutes   **BAKE:** 25 minutes
STAND: 10 minutes

- 1 **pound ground beef**
- 1 **teaspoon dried oregano leaves, crushed**
- ¾ **cup PACE® Picante Sauce**
- 1 **can (about 8 ounces) tomato sauce**
- 1 **can (about 16 ounces) whole kernel corn, drained**
- ½ **cup shredded Cheddar cheese (2 ounces)**
- 1 **package (about 8 ounces) corn muffin mix**

1. Cook the beef and oregano in a 10-inch skillet over medium-high heat until the beef is well browned, stirring often to separate the meat. Pour off any fat.

2. Stir the picante sauce, tomato sauce and corn in the skillet. Cook until the mixture is hot and bubbling. Stir in the cheese. Pour the beef mixture into a 2-quart shallow baking dish.

3. Mix the corn muffin mix according to the package directions. Spread the batter over the beef mixture.

4. Bake at 375°F. for 25 minutes or until the crust is golden brown. Let stand for 10 minutes before serving.

Beef 'n' Bean Bake

MAKES: 4 servings   **PREP:** 10 minutes   **BAKE:** 30 minutes

- 1 **pound ground beef**
- 1 **can (19 ounces) CAMPBELL'S® CHUNKY™ Roadhouse-Beef & Bean Chili**
- ¾ **cup PACE® Picante Sauce**
- ¾ **cup water**
- 8 **corn tortillas (6-inch), cut into 1-inch pieces**
- ⅔ **cup shredded Cheddar cheese**

1. Heat the oven to 400°F.

2. Cook the beef in a 10-inch skillet over medium-high heat until well browned, stirring often to separate the meat. Pour off any fat.

3. Stir the chili, picante sauce, water, tortillas and **half** the cheese in the skillet. Pour the beef mixture into a 2-quart shallow baking dish. Cover the baking dish.

4. Bake for 30 minutes or until the mixture is hot and bubbling. Sprinkle with the remaining cheese.

Baked Pork Chops with Garden Stuffing

MAKES: 6 servings   **PREP:** 15 minutes   **BAKE:** 40 minutes

- 1 **can (10¾ ounces) CAMPBELL'S® Condensed Golden Mushroom Soup**
- ¾ **cup water**
- 1 **bag (16 ounces) frozen vegetable combination (broccoli, cauliflower, carrots)**
- 1 **tablespoon butter**
- 4 **cups PEPPERIDGE FARM® Herb Seasoned Stuffing**
- 6 **bone-in pork chops, ¾-inch thick (about 2 pounds)**

1. Heat the oven to 400°F.

2. Heat ⅓ **cup** soup, ½ **cup** water, vegetables and butter in a 3-quart saucepan over medium-high heat to a boil. Remove the saucepan from the heat. Add the stuffing and mix lightly. Spoon the stuffing mixture into a greased 3-quart baking dish. Arrange the pork on the stuffing.

3. Stir the remaining soup and remaining water in a small bowl. Spoon the soup mixture over the pork.

4. Bake for 40 minutes or until the pork is cooked through.

||||**tip**|||||||||||||||||||||||||||||||||||||||

*You can try varying the vegetable combination **or** the stuffing flavor for a different spin on this recipe.*

Polenta Sausage Bake

MAKES: 8 servings   **PREP:** 20 minutes   **BAKE:** 25 minutes

- 24 **ounces prepared polenta, cut into ½-inch-thick slices**
- ¼ **cup grated Parmesan cheese**
- 1 **pound sweet *or* hot Italian pork sausage, casings removed**
- 1 **large zucchini, cut in half lengthwise and sliced (about 2 cups)**
- 2 **cups PREGO® Traditional Italian Sauce *or* Roasted Garlic & Herb Italian Sauce**
- 6 **ounces shredded fontina *or* mozzarella cheese (about 1½ cups)**

1. Heat the oven to 400°F. Arrange the polenta slices to cover the bottom of a 3-quart shallow baking dish, trimming the slices as needed to fit. Sprinkle with the Parmesan cheese.

2. Cook the sausage in a 12-inch skillet over medium-high heat until it's well browned, stirring often to separate the meat. Remove the sausage from the skillet. Pour off any fat.

3. Add the zucchini to the skillet and cook for 3 minutes or until it's tender. Stir in the Italian sauce and heat to a boil. Return the sausage to the skillet. Cook until the mixture is hot and bubbling. Spoon the sausage mixture over the polenta. Top with the fontina cheese.

4. Bake for 25 minutes or until hot and the cheese is melted.

Broccoli Bake

MAKES: 6 servings   **PREP:** 10 minutes   **BAKE:** 30 minutes

1 can (10¾ ounces) CAMPBELL'S® Condensed Cream of Mushroom Soup (Regular *or* 98% Fat Free)

½ cup milk

1 teaspoon soy sauce

   Generous dash ground black pepper

2 packages (10 ounces *each*) frozen broccoli cuts *or* 4 cups fresh broccoli florets, cooked and drained

1 can (2.8 ounces) French fried onions (about 1⅓ cups)

1. Stir the soup, milk, soy sauce, black pepper, broccoli and ⅔ **cup** onions in a 1½-quart casserole.

2. Bake at 350°F. for 25 minutes or until it's hot and bubbling. Stir the mixture.

3. Top with the remaining onions. Bake for 5 minutes or until the onions are golden.

tips

The recipe may be doubled. Use a 2-quart shallow baking dish and increase the baking time to 30 minutes plus 5 minutes.

You can also use CAMPBELL'S® Condensed Cream of Broccoli Soup, for even more broccoli flavor, in place of the Cream of Mushroom Soup.

Fall Confetti Oven Baked Risotto

MAKES: 6 servings   **PREP:** 5 minutes   **BAKE:** 50 minutes

- 1 can (10¾ ounces) CAMPBELL'S® Condensed Cream of Chicken with Herbs Soup
- 3¼ cups water
- 1¼ cups *uncooked* regular long-grain white rice
- 1 small carrot, shredded (about ⅓ cup)
- ¼ cup frozen peas
- ⅓ cup grated Parmesan cheese

1. Stir the soup, water, rice, carrot and peas in a 2-quart casserole. **Cover**.

2. Bake at 375°F. for 50 minutes or until rice is tender. Stir in the cheese. (Risotto will absorb liquid as it stands.)

Ham and Asparagus Strata

MAKES: 8 servings	PREP: 15 minutes	BAKE: 45 minutes	STAND: 5 minutes

  4 cups PEPPERIDGE FARM® Cubed Country Style Stuffing
  2 cups shredded Swiss cheese (about 8 ounces)
1½ cups cooked cut asparagus
1½ cups cubed cooked ham
  1 can (10¾ ounces) CAMPBELL'S® Condensed Cream of
      Asparagus Soup *or* Condensed Cream of Mushroom Soup
  2 cups milk
  5 eggs
  1 tablespoon Dijon-style mustard

1. Heat the oven to 350°F. Stir the stuffing, cheese, asparagus and ham in a greased 3-quart shallow baking dish.

2. Beat the soup, milk, eggs and mustard in a medium bowl with a fork or whisk. Pour over the stuffing mixture. Stir and press the stuffing mixture into the milk mixture to coat.

3. Bake for 45 minutes or until a knife inserted in the center comes out clean. Let stand for 5 minutes.

tip

*For **1½ cups** cooked cut asparagus, use **¾ pound** fresh asparagus, trimmed and cut into 1-inch pieces **or 1 package** (about 10 ounces) frozen asparagus spears, thawed, drained and cut into 1-inch pieces.*

Greek Rice Bake

MAKES: 6 servings	**PREP:** 15 minutes	**BAKE:** 40 minutes	**STAND:** 5 minutes

- 1 can (10¾ ounces) CAMPBELL'S® Condensed Cream of Mushroom Soup (Regular *or* 98% Fat Free)
- ½ cup water
- 1 can (about 14.5 ounces) diced tomatoes, undrained
- 1 jar (6 ounces) marinated artichoke hearts, drained and cut in half
- 2 portobello mushrooms, coarsely chopped (about 2 cups)
- ¾ cup *uncooked* quick-cooking brown rice
- 1 can (about 15 ounces) small white beans, rinsed and drained
- 3 to 4 tablespoons crumbled feta cheese

1. Heat the oven to 400°F. Stir the soup, water, tomatoes, artichokes, mushrooms, rice and beans in a 2-quart casserole. Cover the casserole.

2. Bake for 40 minutes or until the rice is tender. Stir the rice mixture. Let stand for 5 minutes. Sprinkle with the cheese before serving.

tip

Different brands of quick-cooking brown rice cook differently, so the bake time for this recipe may be slightly longer or shorter than indicated.

Swiss Vegetable Casserole

MAKES: 4 servings   **PREP:** 5 minutes   **BAKE:** 45 minutes

1 can (10¾ ounces) CAMPBELL'S® Condensed Cream of Mushroom Soup (Regular *or* 98% Fat Free)

⅓ cup sour cream

¼ teaspoon ground black pepper

1 bag (16 ounces) frozen vegetable combination (broccoli, cauliflower, carrots), thawed

1 can (2.8 ounces) French fried onions (about 1⅓ cups)

½ cup shredded Swiss cheese

1. Stir soup, sour cream, black pepper, vegetables, ⅔ **cup** onions and ¼ **cup** cheese in 2-quart casserole. Cover casserole.

2. Bake at 350°F. for 40 minutes or until the vegetables are tender. Stir the vegetable mixture. Top with the remaining onions and cheese.

3. Bake for 5 minutes or until the cheese is melted.

For Cheddar Cheese Lovers: Use Cheddar cheese instead of Swiss cheese.

tip

If you like, stir 1 jar (4 ounces) chopped pimientos, drained, into the vegetable mixture before baking.